Missa O Magnum Mysterium
for
Four Voices
by
Victoria

Edited and arranged for modern use by
Henry Washington

CHESTER MUSIC
(A division of Music Sales Limited)
14/15 Berners Street, London, W1T 3LJ

PREFACE

The date of Tomás Luis de Victoria's birth is still uncertain. Early records placed it at between 1535 and 1540, but more recent studies have suggested a date around 1548. His place of birth remains unknown. It is likely, however, that he came from the vicinity of Àvila where his forbears had lived and prospered for several generations. Beyond doubt he was for a time well acquainted with the holy Saint Teresa of Àvila, and as a boy of about ten years of age he was accepted as chorister at Àvila Cathedral. When his voice broke he was sent to Rome to complete his musical studies at the Collegium Germanicum where he subsequently became Maestro di Cappella. He was ordained priest at the comparatively early age of twenty-seven, and held numerous appointments in Rome where he succeeded Palestrina as Maestro di Cappella at the neighbouring Collegium Romanum. Whether there was any master-puil relationship between the two is open to question, but Victoria's compositions often reflect the influence of the great Roman master. It has often been said that Victoria spent most of his musical life in Rome. Nevertheless, he frequently revisited his native Spain, where he spent his last years in Madrid as organist to the convent of the Descalsez Reales, there to seek a life of contemplation until his death in 1611.

The present work, *Missa O Magnum Mysterium*, a Missa Parodia, is based, somewhat slenderly perhaps, on the composer's own beautiful Christmas Motet of similar title,* though Gustave Reese points out a striking reference to the opening of the motet in the Sanctus of this Mass.

It is of interest that among Victoria's twenty known Mass compositions he frequently omits the *Dona nobis pacem* in the Agnus Dei. At the Basilica of Saint John Lateran it was traditional to conclude the Agnus Dei with a third invocation of *Miserere nobis*, a custom which prevailed until recently in the Graduale Romanum for the Mass of Maundy Thursday. On the other hand, notably in his *Missa Simile est Regnum Coelorum*, Victoria surpasses the accepted Roman manner of Mass composition by setting a third Agnus Dei, doubling the previous four parts to eight, and including a quadruple canon.

In this edition the music text is set out unencumbered with arbitrary marks of expression. Thus while the Director is free to insert such guides to performance as he may think expedient, singers are spared the confusion induced by his insistence on say a *pianissimo* reading when an edited score demands a contrary effect.

The sign ⌐ , a short vertical stroke placed above or below a note, is here used freely with the two-fold object of defending verbal rhythm against the accentual power associated with the modern bar-line, and of defining the true agogic accent where an original long note has been replaced by two tied notes of shorter duration. Sixteenth-century note-values have been halved to accord with later acceptance of the crotchet as the normal unit of time.

The present editor is responsible for underlaying the verbal text in accordance with sixteenth-century practice. It should be noted that the final E in the words *Kyrie* and *Christe* is sometimes to be elided. In this edition the elision is indicated by printing the appropriate syllables in italics. If *Dona nobis pacem* is required in the Agnus Dei, this invocation may easily replace the given *Miserere nobis*, as the syllables and accents exactly correspond.

*Available from Chester Music

AMERSHAM
February, 1975

Henry Washington.

MISSA O MAGNUM MYSTERIUM

KYRIE

VICTORIA
Edited by
HENRY WASHINGTON

Ký - ri - e e - léi - - son,

Ký - ri - e e - léi - - son, _____ Ký -

e - léi - - son, Ký - ri - e e - léi - -

Ký - ri - e e - lé - -

f

Ký - ri - e e - léi - - son.

- ri - e e - léi - - - - son.

- - son, Ký - ri - e e - léi - - son.

- - i - son, Ký - ri - e e - léi - - son.

Allargando

GLORIA

CREDO

85

-tum San-ctum Dó-mi - num, et vi-vi-fi - cán - tem: Qui ex Pa - tre Fi - li-ó-

Spí - ri - tum San-ctum Dó - mi - num, et vi - vi-fi-cán - tem: _____ Qui ex

Spí - ri - tum San-ctum Dó - mi - num, et vi - vi-fi-cán - tem: Qui ex·

Spí - ri - tum San-ctum Dó - mi - num, et vi - vi-fi-cán-tem:Qui ex Pa - tre Fi - li-ó-

90

- que pro-cé - dit. Qui cum Pa - tre et Fí - li - o si-mul

Pa - tre Fi - li-ó que pro-cé - dit. Qui cum Pa-tre et Fí - li - o si-mul

Pa - tre Fi - li-ó que pro-cé - dit. Qui cum Pa-tre et Fí - li - o si-mul

- que pro-cé - dit, pro-cé - dit. Si-mul

22

SANCTUS

BENEDICTUS

AGNUS DEI

Printed and bound in Great Britain by
Caligraving Limited Thetford Norfolk

The Chester Books of Madrigals
Edited by Anthony G. Petti

The Chester Books of Madrigals offer an exciting collection of secular European madrigals, partsongs and rounds from the 16th and early 17th centuries, newly edited from early sources by Anthony G. Petti, who contributes copious historical notes to each volume.

The majority of the settings are for SATB, and simplified keyboard reductions with suggested tempi and dynamics are provided as a rehearsal aid or as a basis for a continuo part where appropriate. Texts are in the original languages, English, French, German, Italian and Spanish, with modernised spelling and punctuation. In the case of the non-English texts translations are provided at the head of each piece.

An important feature of this anthology is the arrangement by subjects, which, it is hoped, should be of great assistance in programme planning. Indispensable popular works are interspersed with relatively unfamiliar but attractive and singable pieces.

Les Livres de Madrigaux de Chester proposent une collection très intéressante de madrigaux européens, de chansons à plusieurs voix et de canons des 16° et 17° siècles, récemment éditée par Anthony G. Petti qui s'est inspiré de sources anciennes et qui apporte d'abondantes annotations historiques à chaque volume.

La majorité sont écrits pour chœur à quatre voix mixtes et nous présentons des parties de piano pour répétition avec des suggestions de tempi et de dynamique afin d'aider la répétition ou comme base pour *continuo* si nécessaire. Les textes sont dans la langue d'origine, anglais, français, allemand, italien et espagnol, avec une orthographe et une ponctuation modernes. Pour les textes qui ne sont pas en anglais, des traductions figurent en tête de chaque morceau.

Une caractéristique importante de cette anthologie est la présentation par thèmes qui devrait faciliter l'organisation du programme. Des œuvres populaires célèbres côtoient de beaux morceaux relativement inconnus et agréables à chanter.

Die Chester Books of Madrigals *bieten eine interessante Sammlung weltlicher Madrigale, Kanons und anderer mehrstimmiger Lieder aus dem 16. und frühen 17. Jahruhundert, herausgegeben anhand früher Quellen von Anthony G. Petti, der jedem Band umfassende geschichtliche Beiträge vorangestellt hat.*

Der größte Teil der Chorsätze ist für SATB. Hinzugefügt wurde ein leichter Klaviersatz mit Tempovorschlägen und dynamischen Angaben für die Probenarbeit oder als Grundlage für eine Continuostimme, dort wo sie passend erscheint. Alle Texte sind in der Originalsprache wiedergegeben, englisch, französisch, deutsch, italienisch und spanisch, in zeitgemäßer Schreibweise und Zeichensetzung. Übersetzungen der nicht englischen Texte sind den jeweiligen Liedern vorangestellt.

Ein wichtiges Merkmal dieser Anthologie ist die Aufteilung nach Themen, was eine große Hilfe bei der Programmgestaltung sein sollte. Unentbehrliche bekannte Werke sind vermischt mit relativ unbekannten aber interessanten und singbaren Stücken.

Los Libros Chester de Madrigales ofrecen una interesante colección de madrigales europeos y canciones a varias voces del siglo XVI y principios del siglo XVII, recientemente recopilados de manuscritos originales por Anthony G. Petti, quien enriquece con numerosas notas históricas cada volumen.

La mayoría de las canciones son para 4 voces S.A.T.B. y las reducciones para voces y teclado se ofrecen con tiempos y dinámicas sugeridos, como base o ayuda para ser interpretados con bajo continuo.

Los textos están en los idiomas originales, inglés, francés, alemán, italiano o español, con puntuación y escritura modernas. En el caso de los textos no ingleses se facilitan las traducciones a la cabecera de cada página.

Un logro importante de esta antología es el orden por temas, que esperamos sea de gran ayuda en la planificación de programas. Las obras populares imprescindibles se intercalan con otras relativamente poco conocidas pero muy atractivas.

An index covering Books 1 - 8 is printed in Book 8

Chester Music Limited